The
Ins and Outs
of a
Sex Scene

Cara Knight

The Ins and Outs of a Sex Scene

First published in 2020
© Cara Knight 2020

The right of Cara Knight to be identified as the author of this work has been asserted in accordance with the Copyright, Designs and Patents Act 1988.

All rights reserved. No part of this publication may be reproduced, stored in a retrieval system or transmitted in any form or by any means, without the prior permission in writing of the publisher, nor to be otherwise circulated in any form of binding or cover other than that in which it is published without a similar condition, including this condition, being imposed on the subsequent purchaser.

Cover illustrations © Cara Knight 2020

The Ins and Outs of a Sex Scene

Contents

Introduction 4
Bodies 6
Skin 9
Breasts 10
Nipples 13
Chest 16
Abdomen/ Waist 18
Shoulders 19
Arms 20
Hands & Fingers 22
Buttocks 25
Hips 27
Legs & Feet 29
Back 31
Muscles 32
Face & Neck 33
Eyes 36
Mouth & Lips 37
Tongue 40
Hair 41
Female Genitalia 43
Male Genitalia 47
Having Sex 52
Touch 54
Internal sensations 56
Feelings & Emotions 59
Kissing 62
Penetration 66
Motion during intercourse 69
Female Orgasm 75
Male Orgasm 81
Breathing 86
Sounds 89
Scents & Tastes 90
Places to have sexual encounters 94
Clothing & Toys 99

The Ins and Outs of a Sex Scene

Introduction

By nature, this work contains language some people might find offensive. But let's hope if you've bought the book, you're not easily offended, and I'll assume you're interested rather than appalled by the colorful and scintillating language.

It struck me when reading love scenes and sex scenes that no matter how original the writing, the basic components remain the same. To this end, I compiled this book as a reference guide for authors. All terms should be used with judgment and in harmony with your own writing style and steam level. You should exercise your imagination and creativity to mix and match phrases, words, actions, sensations, body parts, and places to create an explosive cocktail of a scene! I don't claim this work as comprehensive, but hopefully, it will be a useful compendium when writing those saucy scenes.

You will see from the contents, there is a wide range of sections. Some of these overlap, and there is inevitably some repetition. In sections where the same actions may be applied as in other places, I have put them in both. This is to save flicking back and forward. For example, things one can do with breasts may have crossovers to things one can do with nipples, skin, etc. I have attempted to lay it out as simply as possible, though you can of course jump from place to place to whatever section you happen to need inspiration for!

I have also attempted to keep gender to a minimum and avoid stereotyping. You decide who does what with whom. From a purely anatomical standpoint, some sections are divided into male and female, or suggestions are given.

There are of course many other things that human beings can feel, do, and have done to them, however in the context of this book, only the ones with some pertinence to a sex or love scene are mentioned. E.g. Legs can run, jump, and pedal bikes, but they are not common actions for a love scene, so they don't get a mention in this book!

Good luck and happy writing!

If you enjoy this book, please leave a review, and recommend it to your writing friends.

Bodies

Ways to describe bodies more commonly associated with males:

- beefy
- brawny
- broad
- buff
- burly
- dominant
- firm
- fit
- god-like
- hard
- hard-planed
- heavy
- heavy-built
- Herculean
- hot
- hulking
- irresistible
- lanky
- large
- lean
- lithe
- long-legged
- long-limbed
- magnificent
- male
- manly
- meaty
- powerful
- proud
- rampant
- rock hard
- sexy
- sleek
- slender
- solid
- stocky
- stout
- strapping
- strong
- tanned
- taut
- thickset
- toned
- towering

The Ins and Outs of a Sex Scene

- trim
- warm
- well-built
- wiry

Ways to describe bodies more commonly associated with females:

- ample
- angular
- busty
- buxom
- compact
- curvy
- dainty
- elfin
- firm
- fit
- hot
- hourglass-figured
- irresistible
- lanky
- large
- lean
- leggy
- lithe
- long-legged
- long-limbed
- magnificent
- petite
- proud
- sexy
- shapely
- sleek
- slender
- slight
- slim
- statuesque
- strong
- svelte
- tanned
- taut
- toned
- trim
- voluptuous
- warm
- willowy
- wiry

Skin

Ways to describe skin:

- alabaster
- bare
- black
- bronze
- brown
- buck naked
- burning
- covered in beads of sweat
- creamy
- elastic
- fine
- flamed
- flushed
- glistening
- glowing
- heated
- hot
- inflamed
- ivory
- milky
- naked
- olive
- pale
- peachy
- perfect
- pink
- rosy
- satin
- shimmering
- shiny
- silky
- slippery
- smooth
- soft
- sun-warm
- sweat coated
- sweaty
- taut
- tender
- tingling
- velvet
- vulnerable
- warm
- wet

Breasts

Other words for breasts:

- boobs
- bosom
- bust
- chest
- cleavage

Ways to describe breasts:

- aching
- ample
- bare
- bared
- beautifully formed/ shaped
- big
- blossoming
- bouncy
- brazen
- burgeoning
- burning
- creamy
- eager
- exposed
- firm
- flushed
- free
- full
- glistening
- hard
- hardening
- heavy
- jiggling
- jutting
- large
- lush
- magnificent
- naked
- pale
- peachy

- pendant
- perfectly formed/ shaped
- perky
- pert
- pink-tipped
- plump
- rosy
- round
- rounded
- sensitive
- shimmering
- small
- soft
- suspended
- swollen
- taut
- tender
- throbbing
- thrusting
- voluptuous

Things to do to or with breasts

- arouse
- bare
- capture
- caress
- catch
- chart
- circle
- clasp
- crush
- cup
- expose
- fondle
- free
- grasp
- kiss
- knead
- lap
- lick
- massage
- mold
- nuzzle
- palm
- plump
- press

- reshape
- rub
- scoop
- squash
- squeeze
- stroke
- suck
- suckle
- taste
- taunt
- tease
- test the weight of
- take
- warm

Things breasts can do

- ache
- bounce
- bulge
- burn
- burst free
- dangle
- fall
- graze (against body parts)
- harden
- heave
- jiggle
- jut out
- move
- protrude
- quiver
- rise
- skim (over body parts)
- spill
- strain
- surge
- swell
- throb
- thrust
- tighten
- tingle
- wobble

Nipples

Other words for nipples:

- areolas
- buds
- centers
- crests
- nubs
- peaks
- pebbles
- points
- tips
- tits

Ways to describe nipples:

- aching
- bare
- beaded
- delectable
- delicate
- dimpled
- distended
- engorged
- erect
- flushed
- hard
- hardened
- heated
- little
- peaked
- pearled
- pebbled
- perky
- pert
- petite
- pink
- plump

- pointed
- protruding
- proud
- pulsing
- quivering
- rigid
- ripe
- rock-like
- rosy
- sensitive
- shimmering
- small
- stiff
- swollen
- taut
- tender
- throbbing
- ticklish
- tight
- tingling
- turgid
- velvet
- waiting
- wet

Things to do with nipples

- brush across
- capture
  - between lips
  - between teeth
- caress
- circle
- flick
- flick tongue over
- graze
  - with fingertips
  - with lips
  - with teeth
  - with other body parts
- knead
- lash
- lick
- nibble
- pinch
- probe

- rasp
- roll
- rub
- shape
- suck
- suckle
- take
  - between fingertips
  - between teeth
  - in one's mouth
  - with one's lips
- taste
- tease
- touch
- tug
- wet
- whisk with tongue

Things nipples can do:

- ache
- grow
  - erect
  - large
  - rigid
- harden
- peak
- pucker
- push (against skin/ clothes)
- rise
- shiver
- spring to attention
- strain
- swell
- tauten
- tense
- throb
- tighten
- tingle

Chest

Although many of these words/ phrases are gender-neutral, some more frequently lend themselves to male anatomy (female chests are well-covered under breasts!)

Other words for the chest:

- pecs
- pectorals
- sternum
- torso
- trunk

Ways to describe the male chest:

- a curved ridge of pecs
- barrelled
- beefy
- broad
- carved
- contoured
- covered in a smattering of hair
- etched
- flat
- hair-encircled nipples
- hairless
- hair-roughened skin
- hairy
- hard
- heavy
- muscular

- rippling pecs
- sculpted
- shapely
- smooth lines
- solid wall
- taut
- toned
- virile
- well-honed
- with a trail of hair

Things to do to or with the chest:

- bare
- brush across
- caress
- chart
- circle
- explore
- expose
- feel
- feel up
- flick one's tongue over
- kiss
- lap
- lick
- massage
- nibble
- nuzzle
- press
- rub
- stroke
- suck
- taste
- touch
- touch up
- wet
- whisk with tongue

Abdomen/ Waist

Other words for the abdomen and its parts:

- abs
- belly
- love handles
- middle
- midriff
- navel
- six-pack
- stomach
- tum
- tummy
- waist
- waistline

Ways to describe the abdomen:

Descriptions more commonly used with males are marked (m) and females (f). Exercise your own writer's judgment on how they will work with your characters.

- corrugated
- curvy (f)
- dainty (f)
- flat
- flexible
- full
- hard ridges
- hard slab
- lean
- line of hair leading to the navel (m)
- lithe
- muscled flesh
- narrow
- plump
- sculpted
- sensitive
- slender
- slim
- structured
- supple
- tapering
- taut
- tight
- toned
- well-defined
- well-honed

Shoulders

Parts of the shoulder:

- clavicle
- collarbone
- scapula
- shoulder blade

Ways to describe shoulders:

- angular
- bony
- broad
- bunching
- contoured
- hard
- hulking
- muscled
- muscular
- narrow
- powerful
- prominent
- robust
- rounded with muscle
- sharp
- sleek
- skinny
- square
- strong
- taut
- tense
- well-set
- wide

Arms

Parts of the arm:

- armpits
- biceps
- elbows
- forearms
- hands (see separate entry on hands & Fingers)
- muscles
- upper arm
- wrists

Ways to describe arms:

Some of these descriptions lend themselves particularly to biceps!

- brawny
- bulging
- firm
- flexed
- flexible
- graceful
- limber
- muscled
- powerful
- strong
- taut
- tight

Things arms can do:

- brace (oneself/ one's partner/ body parts)
- bracket
- cage
- clasp
- clinch
- cuddle
- drape
- embrace
- enfold
- hold
- hold hands above head (one's own or one's partner's)
- hug
- lift
- position
- prop (on arm(s)/ elbows etc)
- raise over one's head
- squeeze
- support
- take the weight
- wrap around

Hands & Fingers

Parts of the hand:

- fingers
- fingertips
- knuckles
- nails
- pad of thumb
- palm
- thumbs

Ways to describe hands/ fingers:

- bold
- bony
- calloused
- capable
- clumsy
- cold
- confident
- dainty
- deft
- delicate
- eager
- excited
- frantic
- fumbling
- huge
- large
- lithe
- neat
- nimble
- powerful
- precise
- rough
- shaky
- skilled
- skinny
- slender
- small
- smooth

- sophisticated
- strong
- thin
- trembling
- uncertain
- veined
- warm

Things hands/ fingers can do:

- arouse
- brush
- brush across
- caress
- chart
- circle
- clasp
- clench
- clinch
- cling
- clutch
- crush
- dig into
- expose
- feel
- feel up
- fist
- flex
- flick
- fondle
- free
- frisk
- grasp
- graze
- grip
- handle
- insert
- knead
- mark skin (with nails)
- massage
- mold
- open (clothes/ legs etc)
- palm
- pat
- pet
- pinch

- play around
- plump
- position
- press
- probe
- pull
- push
- push up
- rub
- scoop
- score (with nails)
- skate
- slap
- smack
- squash
- squeeze
- stimulate
- stroke
- take
- take clothes off (self or partner)
- taste
- taunt
- tease
- tickle
- touch
- touch up
- toy
- trail
- tug
- unbutton
- undress
- unzip
- warm
- work on
- wrap

Buttocks

Other words for buttocks and parts of the buttock:

- arse
- ass
- backside
- bottom
- bum
- butt
- cheek
- crack
- rear
- rump

Ways to describe buttocks:

- ample
- bare
- beefy
- curvy
- flat
- hard
- lithe
- perfect
- pert
- plump
- round
- smooth
- supple
- taut
- tight

Things to do to or with buttocks:

- brush across
- caress
- chart
- circle
- clinch
- clutch
- cup
- dig fingers into
- expose
- feel
- feel up
- flick one's tongue over
- fondle
- grasp
- graze
- grope
- handle
- kiss
- knead
- lap
- lash
- lick
- massage
- mold
- nibble
- nuzzle
- pat
- pet
- pinch
- plump
- press
- probe
- rub
- slap
- smack
- squash
- squeeze
- stroke
- tease
- touch
- touch up
- warm
- wet
- whisk with tongue

Hips

Ways to describe hips:

- bony
- boyish
- broad
- curved
- curvy
- feminine
- flexible
- full
- generous
- graceful
- lean
- lithe
- manly
- masculine
- narrow
- plump
- prominent
- rotund
- sensual
- sleek
- slender
- slim
- straight
- sturdy
- supple
- tapered
- tiny
- undulating
- well-rounded
- wide

Action words/ phrases for hips:

- bracing against
- grinding
- gyrating
- jolting
- juddering
- lifting hips (from a mattress/ bed/ table etc.)
- lifting partner by hips
- opening
- picking up partner's hips
- positioning
- pumping
- raising hips
- rolling hips
- rotating
- screwing
- shuddering
- sitting astride
- slamming
- straddling
- thrusting
- tilting
- tipping one's hips
- vibrating
- wiggling
- wriggling

Legs & Feet

Parts of the leg & feet:
- ankles
- calves
- feet
- heels
- knees
- leg hair
- shins
- thighs
- toenails
- toes

Ways to describe legs:
- elegant
- flexible
- hairy
- lean
- like tree trunks
- limber
- lithe
- long
- muscular
- nimble
- powerful
- shaky
- shapely
- short
- skinny
- slender
- smooth
- spindly
- sturdy
- supple
- tanned
- taut thighs
- trembling

Action words and phrases pertaining to legs:

- bringing knees up to accommodate (partner's cock, fingers, tongue, etc.)
- clamping legs around partner
- draping legs over
- feeling body fluids dripping on thighs
- hooking knees over partner's arms
- hooking legs around partner's waist
- kneeling between partner's thighs
- kneeling in position
- locking ankles behind partner
- massaging heels/ balls of feet
- placing feet on partners shoulders/ chest/ thighs
- positioning legs
- sitting on partner's legs
- splaying legs
- spreading legs
- sucking toes
- using one's knee to open partner for penetration
- wrapping legs around

Back

Other words for the back & parts of the back:

- backbone
- small of back
- spinal cord
- spine
- vertebrae

Ways to describe the back:

- arched
- bare
- beefy
- bony
- brawny
- brittle
- broad
- carved
- curvaceous
- delicate
- elegant
- etched
- feline
- firm
- hairy
- impressive
- muscled planes
- powerful
- ramrod-straight
- rigid
- smooth
- solid
- straight
- sturdy
- supple
- taut
- tender
- tight
- toned
- tough
- trim

Muscles

Ways to describe muscles:

- brittle
- bunching
- corded
- elastic
- fine
- fleshy
- flexible
- gnarled
- hard
- hard-edged
- having a solid muscular frame
- having fine musculature
- knotted
- lean
- massive
- powerful
- rigid
- rippling
- rock-hard
- rope-like
- sinewy
- sleek
- smooth
- solid
- steely
- stiff
- strained ridges
- strong
- sturdy
- supple
- swollen
- tapered
- taut
- tense
- tight
- tough
- well-defined
- wiry

Face & Neck

Parts of the face and neck:

- Adam's apple
- beard
- brows
- cheekbones
- cheeks
- chin
- dimples
- earlobes
- ears
- eyebrows (see separate entry on eyes)
- eyelashes (see separate entry on eyes)
- eyes (see separate entry on eyes)
- forehead
- glasses
- head
- irises (see separate entry on eyes)
- jaw
- jawbone
- lips (see separate entry on mouth & lips)
- mustache
- mouth (see separate entry on mouth & lips)

- neck
- nose
- nostrils
- pupils (see separate entry on eyes)
- stubble
- teeth (see separate entry on mouth & lips)
- temple
- throat

Ways to describe the face and neck:

- abrasive (facial hair)
- attractive
- beautiful
- cheeky
- clean-shaven
- flushed
- forehead beaded with sweat
- gorgeous
- handsome
- hard outline of jaw
- pleasant
- sexy
- smiling
- stubble-coated jaw
- stunning

Things faces and necks can do:

Some pertain more to certain parts than others – Eg: you might tug on an earlobe but not necessarily a mustache (though who knows?)

- be exposed
- blush
- drop (neck) backward
- flush
- have a partner's tongue flicked over (cheeks, neck, etc.)
- kiss (see separate entry on kissing)
- nudge
- nuzzle
- press
- rub
- throw head back
- touch

Eyes

Parts of the eyes:
- eyebrows
- eyelashes
- eyelid
- irises
- pupils
- white of the eye

Things eyes can do:

- admire
- bat (eyelashes/eyelids)
- blink
- consider
- dilate (pupils)
- eye
- eye-up
- flutter (eyelashes)
- gaze
- give the eye
- give the once over
- glance
- glimpse
- look up and down
- narrow
- observe
- ogle
- raise (eyebrows)
- stare
- take in
- take in
- undress (metaphorically)
- watch
- widen
- wink

Mouth & Lips

Parts of the mouth:
- gums
- lips
- lower lip
- roof of mouth
- saliva
- teeth
- tongue (see separate entry on tongue)
- upper lip

Ways to describe mouths:
- curved
- firm
- generous
- loose
- needy
- open
- ready
- seductive
- sensitive
- sensual
- slack
- smiling
- straight
- tempting
- tender
- wet
- wide

Things mouths can do:

- breathe (see separate entry on breathing)
- give oral sex
- kiss (see separate entry on kissing)
- make
- sounds (see separate entry on sounds)
- open
- salivate
- smile
- take body parts within (cock, nipples, toes, etc.)
- taste

Ways to describe lips:

- alluring
- ample
- beautiful
- desirable
- enticing
- full
- generous
- glittery
- glossy
- heavenly
- honeyed
- hot
- juicy
- kissable
- luscious
- lush
- lusty
- luxurious
- opulent
- peachy
- petit
- pink
- plump
- pouty

- pretty
- red
- rich
- ripe
- rosy
- round
- sensual
- sexy
- smiling
- smooth
- soft
- sparkly
- sugary
- sweet
- swollen
- tasty
- tempting
- tender
- thin
- trembling
- voluptuous
- warm
- wet

Things one can do with lips:

- capture them
- kiss with them (see separate entry on kissing)
- nip them with teeth
- open them
- part them
- sip them
- smack them
- suck them
- suckle them

Tongue

Ways to describe tongues:

- hesitant
- moist
- persuasive
- rough
- seductive
- silky
- warm

Tongues can:

- circle
- curl
- dance
- dart inside
- dive
- encircle
- glide
- invade
- lick
- make swirling motions
- mate
- part lips
- plunder
- plunge
- quest
- reclaim
- search
- seek
- slide
- slip
- stroke
- sweep inside
- tangle
- thrust
- twine

Hair

Ways to describe hair:

Describing hair could be a work in itself. I have given a few ideas to describe hair that would appeal during a sex scene.

- beautiful
- bouncy
- bristly
- cascading
- clean
- clipped
- combed
- conditioned
- curly
- damp
- delicate
- feathery
- fine
- flowing
- fluffy
- freshly washed
- frizzy
- gelled
- gleaming
- glossy
- luscious
- shiny
- silky
- spiky
- thick
- untamed
- velvety
- voluminous
- wavy
- wet
- wild

Things to do to or with hair:

- anchoring hands/ fingers in hair
- entwining fingers in partner's hair
- fisting hair
- hair falling (over body, edge of bed, etc.)
- hair spilling
- knotting fingers in partner's hair
- letting hair fall around partner
- letting hair hang over shoulders when straddling partner
- letting hair loose
- piling on top of head
- pulling into ponytail
- rubbing hair over partner
- ruffling hair
- smoothing
- stroking
- tangling hair
- threading fingers in partner's hair
- trailing hair over
- wrapping hair (around hands/ neck)
- working fingers through hair

Female Genitalia

Words and phrases for female genitalia:

- apex of her legs
- bare flesh
- between
    - her hips
    - her legs
    - her thighs
- center
- cleft between her legs
- clit
- clitoris
- core
- deeper heat within
- delicate softness
- entrance
- excitement
- flesh
- g-spot
- her heat
- hot pool
- inner thigh
- inside
- juncture of her thighs
- lips

- loins
- mound
- nest of hair
- pelvic floor
- pelvis
- petal
- pussy
- sensitive spot
- slick wet heat
- slickness
- slit
- soft folds
- softness
- stretching walls of her body
- sweet warmth
- sweetness
- tight depths
- warmth between her legs
- wetness
- womanhood

Ways to describe female genitalia:

- damp
- desperate
- engorged
- hot
- moist
- molten
- needy
- receptive
- sensitive
- sheathing
- slick
- slippery
- smooth
- soft
- tender
- tight
- warm
- wet

Things female genitalia can do:
- ache
  - for fulfillment
  - with desperation
  - with need
- drip
- pulsate
- throb

Things you can do to female genitalia:

- arouse
- bring her close
- circle
- close mouth over
- find g-spot
- fist
- frisk
- insert a finger
- insert a thumb
- lap
- lap up
- lick
- massage
- palm
- slide a finger inside
- soothe one's hands over
- suck on
- take into one's mouth
- thrum
- use languid strokes to arouse
- use one's tongue to flick over

Male Genitalia

Words and phrases for male genitalia:
- arousal
- aroused flesh
- balls
- bulge
- cock
- cockhead
- crotch
- dick
- erection
- evidence of his arousal
- flesh
- fullness
- groin
- hardness
- loins
- manhood
- member
- nether regions
- rod
- sack
- scrotum
- sex
- shaft
- testicles

Ways to describe male genitalia:

- aching
- aggressive
- aroused
- blatant
- bulging
- burgeoning
- distended
- eager
- engorged
- erect
- fiery
- firm
- flaccid
- full
- growing
- half-erect
- happy
- hard
- heavy
- hot
- huge
- instant
- iron-hard
- jutting
- magnificent
- massive
- molten
- needy
- over sensitized
- primed
- pulsating
- pulsing
- rapidly growing
- ready
- rigid
- rock hard
- semi-erect
- sinewy
- stirring
- straining
- swelling
- swollen
- thick
- throbbing
- virile

Things male genitalia can do:

- ache
- become erect
- become rigid
- be ready for action
- bob
- bulge
- burst
- come
- ejaculate
- firm up
- grow
- harden
- jerk
- leak
- nudge
- orgasm
- press
- prod
- pulsate
- pulse
- push
- spring free
- stand proud
- stand to attention
- stiffen
- stir
- swell
- tense
- thicken
- throb
- thrust
- twitch

Things you can do to or with male genitalia:

- arouse
- caress
- chart
- clasp
- explore
- feel
  - him hardening against one's (thighs, tummy, tongue, etc.)
  - him pushing against body parts
  - semen flooding (one's mouth, or other places)
- flick one's tongue over
- fondle
- free
- give a blow job
- grasp
- kiss
- lap
- let him hit the back of one's throat (during oral sex)
- lick
- massage
  - between breasts
  - his tip with the back of one's throat
  - with hands or fingers

- move one's mouth over
- mold
- nearly swallow his tip
- perform oral sex
- pleasure
- pump
  - between breasts
  - with one's hands or fingers
- push one's face forward until one's nose and lips press the base of his cock
- rub
- sheath with a condom
- sink down on
- squeeze inside during orgasm
- stroke
- suck
- suction
- swallow
  - his cock
  - his semen
- take
  - him into one's mouth
  - his length
- taste
- touch
- tease

Having Sex

The sex act can also be known as:

- bedding
- fucking
- getting it on
- going to bed
- having it off
- making love
- screwing
- shagging
- sleeping with

Other sexual acts:

- dry humping
- engaging in foreplay
- giving a blowjob
- giving a hand job
- kissing (see separate entry on kissing)
- masturbating
- performing cunnilingus
- performing fellatio
- performing oral sex

Safe sex

- birth control measures
- condoms
- keeping clean

Words relating to sex drive:

- eroticism
- libido
- lust
- passion
- sex drive
- sexual desire
- sexual urge
- sexuality
- the hots

Sexual Positions

- cowgirl
- doggy style
- from behind
- her on top
- him on top
- lifting partner
- missionary
- on a chair
- over a table
- reverse cowgirl
- sitting
- spooning
- standing

Touch

Ways to touch (partner/ oneself/ body parts)

- agitate
- arouse
- brush
- brush across
- caress
- chart
- circle
- clasp
- clinch
- clutch
- coddle
- cosset
- crush
- cuddle
- embrace
- explore
- expose
- feel
- feel up
- fist
- flick
- flick one's tongue over
- fondle
- free
- grasp
- graze
- handle
- hug
- kiss
- knead
- lap
- lash
- lick
- massage
- mold
- nibble
- nuzzle
- palm
- pat
- pet
- pinch
- play around
- plump
- press
- probe

The Ins and Outs of a Sex Scene

- rub
- scoop
- slap
- smack
- snuggle
- squash
- squeeze
- stimulate
- stroke
- suck
- suckle
- take
- taste
- taunt
- tease
- touch
- touch up
- toy
- tug
- warm
- wet
- whisk with tongue

Internal sensations

- adrenaline
  - flooding veins
  - rushing
  - surging
- blood
  - pounding
  - rushing
  - surging
- control
  - ebbing away
  - loss of
- emotional
  - chemistry
  - sparks
  - urges
- heart/ heartbeat
  - doubling
  - increasing
  - pounding
  - quickening
  - racing
  - raging
  - skipping a beat
  - throbbing

- heat
    - building
    - frenzied
    - flashes of
    - increasing
    - rising
    - searing
- nerve-ends
    - heightened
    - prickling
    - tingling
- pulse
    - increasing
    - quickening
    - racing
    - throbbing
    - tingling
    - soaring
- sexual energy
    - intense
    - raw
- temperature
    - rising
    - soaring
- veins
    - surging with adrenaline
    - tingling

Internal sensations may feel:
- achy
- agonizing
- arousing
- boiling
- deep
- desperate
- drunken
- electrifying
- energizing
- exciting
- fluttery
- fun
- hot
- intense
- intoxicating
- invigorating
- needy
- painful
- pleasurable
- raw
- rousing
- stimulating
- sweet
- throbbing
- wanton

Feelings & Emotions

One may feel:

- admiration
- adoration
- amusement
- anticipation
- ardor
- attraction
- conflicted
- curiosity
- delight
- desire
- desperation
- eagerness
- ecstasy
- euphoria
- excitement
- fervor
- fondness
- greed
- happiness
- hunger
- infatuation
- joy
- longing
- love
- lust
- need
- nervousness
- passion
- rapture
- ravenousness
- satisfaction
- thirst
- uncertainty
- vulnerability
- yearning

Ways to describe feelings:

- all-consuming
- ardent
- blazing
- boiling
- burning
- crazy
- deep
- desperate
- eager
- ecstatic
- euphoric
- excited
- extreme
- fervent
- feverish
- fiery
- frenzied
- happy
- hot
- hungry
- intense
- joyful
- loving
- keen
- new
- obsessive
- passionate
- powerful
- raw
- red-hot
- scorching
- sweet
- sweltering
- thrilling

Ways to describe people in a sexy or romantic mood:

- affectionate
- amorous
- charming
- coy
- enthusiastic
- excited
- flirtatious
- flirty
- happy
- having the hots
- infatuated
- kittenish
- loving
- lustful
- passionate
- ready
- sensual
- teasing
- up for anything

Kissing

Other words meaning kissing

- canoodling
- French kissing
- getting off
- making out
- necking
- nuzzling
- pecking
- playing tonsil tennis
- smacking (a smack on the lips)
- smooching
- snogging

Ways to kiss

- absorbing one's partner
- angling head (for better position/ access)
- brushing lips
- capturing
  - partner's lips
  - partner's mouth
- catching
  - partner's lips
  - partner's mouth

- chasing
  - partner's lips
  - partner's mouth
  - partner's tongue
- crashing mouths together
- cupping face in both hands while kissing
- deepening kisses
- exploring
  - partner's lips
  - partner's mouth
  - partner's tongue
- feathering partner's lips
- feeding from partner's mouth
- licking
- mashing lips together
- melding
- melting
- nipping
- nuzzling
- open-mouthed kissing
- plying partner with kisses
- reclaiming partner's mouth
- skimming
- smashing lips together
- sucking
- teasing

Ways to describe kisses:

- deep
- delicious
- delirious
- devastating
- dreamy
- drugging
- engulfing
- erotic
- exploratory
- fast
- featherlight
- feathery
- feverish
- gentle
- hard
- hot
- hungry
- intense
- intoxicating
- languid
- languorous
- lingering
- long
- mindless
- passionate
- pervasive
- probing
- provocative
- quick
- ravaging
- rich
- tough
- savage
- searching
- sensual
- sexy
- slow
- soft
- soulful
- thorough
- urgent

One can kiss:

- deeply
- deliriously
- desperately
- fervently
- feverishly
- fiercely
- gently
- hungrily
- intensely
- mindlessly
- passionately
- provocatively
- quickly
- savagely
- sensually
- slowly
- softly
- soulfully
- thoroughly
- urgently
- voraciously
- with finesse
- with slanting lips
- without finesse

Penetration

For the partner being penetrated, the action can be described as:

- accepting
- easing onto
- enveloping
- gliding onto
- guiding one's partner inside
- lowering oneself
- moving to accept
- relaxing
- screwing oneself down
- sheathing
- sinking down
- sliding down
- straddling
- stretching to accommodate one's partner
- surrendering oneself
- taking one's partner inside
- yielding

For the partner doing the penetration, the action can be described as:

- burying
- claiming
- driving into
- easing oneself inside
- embedding
- entering
- filling
- gliding upward
- grinding into
- guiding partner on top
- holding at the entrance
- inching inside
- moving inside
- gliding into
- imbedding
- impaling
- nudging inside
- penetrating
- plunging into
- possessing
- pressing into
- probing
- pulling partner on top

The Ins and Outs of a Sex Scene

- pumping inside
- pushing in
- sinking in
- sheathing inside partner
- sliding inside
- slipping in
- spearing
- taking
- thrusting inside

When describing the action as a whole:

- coming together
- joining
- merging
- slotting together

Penetration can be done:

- carefully
- completely
- deeply
- fully
- gingerly
- inch by inch
- in one swift motion
- little by little
- slowly
- to the hilt
- with a driving thrust
- with a long thrust
- with ease
- with one deep thrust

Motion during intercourse

Action words for motion:

- answering
  - thrusting hips
  - thrusts
- arching
  - like a cat
  - off the ground/ bed etc
  - one's back
  - one's body
  - one's hips
  - to meet fingers/ hand
  - to meet thrusts
  - to take partner further
  - up/ upward
- bucking
- circling movements
- clenching
- colliding
- delving
- grinding
  - down
  - one's body into partner
- gyrating
- heaving
- increasing strokes

- jerking
- lifting
  - hips
  - one's body
  - partner's body
- matching partner's movements
- meeting thrusts
- moving
  - deeper
  - in response
  - involuntarily
  - simultaneously
  - together
- pounding
- pressing
  - against
  - deeper
  - hips against partner
- pulsating
- pulsing
- pushing
- raising
  - hips
  - one's body against partner
  - one's partner higher
- riding
- rocking

The Ins and Outs of a Sex Scene

- - against partner
  - in unison
  - over and over
- rising
  - against partner's touch
  - to meet partner's thrusts
- rotating hips
- rubbing against partner
- shifting
- shivering
- shuddering
- slamming thrusts
- slapping hips
- squeezing around
- squirming
- sucking in, then releasing
- surging
  - and ebbing
  - repeatedly
  - upward
- swaying
- thrashing
- throbbing
- thrusting
  - hips together
  - into partner
  - one's body

- thundering against partner
- twisting
- undulating
- vibrating
- wriggling
  - hips
  - on partner's lap
- writhing
  - against partner's thighs
  - beneath partner
  - body
  - with need

Other components to consider alongside motion:

- friction
- rhythm
  - calculated
  - in tune
  - increased
  - insistent
  - measured
  - perfect
  - primal
  - pulsing
  - regular
  - sensual
  - stirring
  - swaying

- unconscious
- tempo
    - brisk
    - decreasing
    - deliberate
    - exhilarating
    - fast
    - harsh
    - increasing
    - rapid
    - relentless
    - rhythmical
    - slow
    - speedy

During motion body parts may move/ touch in the following places:

- against
- beneath
- in and out
- inside
- into
- on top of
- over
- under
- upward

Ways to describe motion:

- brisk
- deep
- deliberate
- exhilarating
- fast
- frenetic
- frenzied
- hypnotic
- in perfect rhythm
- insistent
- rapid
- relentless
- rhythmical
- slow
- subtle

Motion can also be done:

- desperately
- frantically
- in a frenzy
- rhythmically
- violently
- wildly

Female Orgasm

Female orgasms can be:

- a crescendo
- a current
- a frenzy
- a peak
- a pinnacle
- a release
- a shudder
- a spasm
- a wave
- an eruption
- an explosion
- an undulation
- contractions

- a chain of
- a crescendo of
- a current/ currents of
- a flood of
- a fountain of
- a frenzy/ frenzies of
- a jolt/ jolts of
- a moment of

- a peak/ peaks of
- a pinnacle of
- a release of
- a ripple/ ripples of
- a rush of
- a sensation of/ sensation of
- a shock/ shocks of
- a shudder/ shudders of
- a spasm/ spasms of
- a thrill/ thrills of
- a tremor/ tremors of
- a wave/ waves of
- an eruption/ eruptions of
- an explosion/ explosions of
- undulations of

(The above phrases can be mixed and matched with the following list. E.g. A flood of ecstasy or waves of delight)

- agony
- bliss
- contentment
- delight
- desire
- ecstasy
- elation
- electricity
- energy
- euphoria
- excitement
- exhilaration
- fever
- frenzy
- fulfillment
- intensity

- joy
- lust
- orgasm
- passion
- pleasure
- rapture
- satisfaction
- tension

Ways to describe the sensations leading up to and during orgasm:

- agonizing
- blinding
- blissful
- blistering
- blood-rushing
- burning
- bursting
- cataclysmic
- clenching
- coiling
- consuming
- convulsive
- dazzling
- deep
- desperate
- devastating
- dizzying
- eager
- ecstatic
- engulfing
- erotic
- exciting
- exhilarating
- explosive
- exquisite
- fervent
- feverish
- fierce
- fiery
- fitful
- fizzing
- flooding
- frantic
- frenetic
- frenzied
- giddy
- glorious
- gushing

- heady
- heavenly
- incredible
- infinite
- intense
- intolerable
- juddering
- multiple
- orgasmic
- overpowering
- overwhelming
- passionate
- perfect
- pleasurable
- powerful
- primal
- profound
- pulsating
- pulsing
- quivering
- rapid
- red-hot
- rhythmic
- rushing
- soaring
- screaming
- sensational
- sensual
- shattering
- sheer
- shimmering
- shuddering
- simultaneous
- soul-shattering
- squirming
- strong
- surging
- sweet
- thrilling
- tight
- total
- trembling
- tremulous
- ultimate
- unbearable
- uncontrollable
- urgent
- wild

Action words for female orgasms:

- to be claimed by... (can be used by adding previous descriptions. E.g. to be claimed by a moment of bliss)
- to be hit by a wave of... (can be used by adding previous descriptions. E.g. to be hit by a wave of pleasure)
- to be pushed over the edge
- to be seized by... (can be used by adding previous descriptions. E.g. to be seized by a spasm of delight)
- to break
- to burst
- to clench
- to climax
- to come
- to contract
- to convulse
- to erupt
- to explode
- to feel ready to pass out/ black out
- to furl/ unfurl
- to orgasm
- to peak
- to quiver
- to reach

The Ins and Outs of a Sex Scene

- to ride out
- to ride the waves of
- to rip through
- to rise
- to soar
- to shudder
- to splinter apart
- to squirm
- to stiffen in… (can be used by adding previous descriptions. E.g. to stiffen in dizzying contentment)
- to tear through
- to thrash

Where these sensations are felt:

- all over
- around one's partner
- below
- deep inside
- into infinity
- shooting through one's body

Male Orgasm

Male orgasms can be:

- a convulsion
- a culmination
- a current
- a frenzy
- a peak
- a release
- a shudder
- a spasm
- a wave
- an eruption
- an explosion
- an undulation

- a bolt/ bolts of
- a flood of
- a fountain of
- a frenzy/ frenzies of
- a jolt/ jolts of
- a lightning bolt/ lightning bolts of
- a moment of
- a peak/ peaks of
- a pinnacle of
- a release of

- a ripple/ ripples of
- a rush of
- a shock/ shocks of
- a shudder/ shudders of
- a spasm/ spasms of
- a thrill/ thrills of
- a tremor/ tremors of
- a wave/ waves of
- an eruption/ eruptions of
- an explosion/ explosions of
- undulations of

(The above phrases can be mixed and matched with the following list. E.g. shocks of exhilaration or an explosion of joy)

- agony
- bliss
- contentment
- delight
- desire
- ecstasy
- elation
- electricity
- energy
- euphoria
- excitement
- exhilaration
- fever
- frenzy
- fulfillment
- intensity
- joy
- lust
- orgasm
- passion
- pleasure
- rapture
- satisfaction
- tension

Ways to describe the sensations leading up to and during orgasm:

- agonizing
- blinding
- blissful
- blistering
- blood-rushing
- burning
- bursting
- cataclysmic
- consuming
- convulsive
- dazzling
- deep
- desperate
- devastating
- dizzying
- eager
- ecstatic
- engulfing
- erotic
- exciting
- exhilarating
- explosive
- feverish
- fierce
- fiery
- final
- fitful
- flooding
- frantic
- frenetic
- frenzied
- giddy
- glorious
- gushing
- heady
- hot
- incredible
- infinite
- intense
- intolerable
- jarring
- juddering
- long
- molten
- orgasmic
- overpowering

- overwhelming
- passionate
- perfect
- pleasurable
- powerful
- primal
- profound
- pulsating
- pulsing
- rapid
- red-hot
- rushing
- sensational
- sensual
- shattering
- sheer
- shuddering
- simultaneous
- soaring
- soul-shattering
- staccato
- strong
- surging
- thrilling
- tight
- total
- ultimate
- unbearable
- uncontrollable
- urgent
- white-hot
- wild

Action words for male orgasms:

- to break
- to buck
- to burst
- to climax
- to come
- to convulse
- to ejaculate
- to erupt
- to explode
- to flood
- to let go
- to lose control
- to peak
- to pour
- to pulsate
- to reach

- to release (oneself)
- to ricochet
- to ride
- to rise
- to rocket
- to shake
- to shudder
- to slam
- to soar
- to spasm
- to spend (oneself)
- to spill
- to stiffen
- to tear through

Where these sensations are felt:

- all over
- below
- deep inside
- inside one's partner
- into infinity
- shooting through one's body
- within

Words that can be used for semen:

- come
- cum
- hot seed
- jazz
- juice
- lava
- seed

Breathing

Words and phrases for breathing:

- feeling as if air is being forced from lungs
- fighting for more oxygen
- gasping
- inhaling/ exhaling
- panting
- pulling in air
- shuddering
- sighing
- sucking air

Breathing can feel:

- agonizing
- choppy
- deep
- erratic
- fast
- fitful
- hard
- harsh
- heavy
- irregular
- jagged
- labored

- low
- quick
- ragged
- rapid
- shallow
- short
- shuddering
- uneven
- unsteady
- urgent
- warm

It can involve taking breaths that:

- are accompanied by a shiver
- are forced
- catch in one's throat
- come in
    - fits and starts
    - punctuated gasps
    - short spurts
- emerge in gasps
- feel
    - hot
    - intense
    - labored
    - moist
- grow short

The Ins and Outs of a Sex Scene

- halt (at partner's touch etc)
- have a desperate rhythm
- hiss
- hurt one's lungs
- quicken
- rush in and out

Sounds

Words and phrases for making sounds:

- begging
- calling out
- crying
- crying out
- crying partner's name
- groaning
- growling
- moaning
- muttering
- pleading
- protesting
- screaming
- shrieking
- squealing
- whimpering
- whispering
- yelling

Ways to describe sounds:

- breathy
- deep
- desperate
- eager
- ecstatic
- feminine
- frantic
- guttural
- harsh
- low
- lustful
- masculine
- needy
- satisfied
- strangled
- unabashed
- wanton

The Ins and Outs of a Sex Scene

Scents & Tastes

Some of these will apply more to one or the other sense, but there are several crossovers, so mix and match as necessary.

Ways to describe scents & tastes:

- aromatic
- arousing
- bitter
- citrussy
- clean
- clear
- cool
- crisp
- delicious
- earthy
- feminine
- floral
- flowery
- fragrant
- fresh
- fruity
- heady
- intoxicating
- leathery
- lemony
- male
- manly
- masculine
- minty
- musky
- natural
- peachy
- perfumed
- pleasant
- raw
- refreshing
- rich
- salty
- sexy
- smoky
- spicy
- sweaty
- sweet
- tangy
- virile
- warm
- woody

Food and Drink considered sensual or attractive:

Either to eat/ drink prior to or during an encounter, as part of an encounter, or as a taste on the lips/ mouth of a partner.

- bananas
- beer
- black pepper
- champagne
- cherries
- chilies
- chocolate
- cocktails
- coke
- cordials
- desserts
- figs
- gin
- grapes
- ice-cream
- liqueurs
- melted chocolate
- oysters
- pomegranates
- prosecco
- salt
- spice
- strawberries
- watermelon
- whipped cream
- whisky
- wine

Products that enhance scents:

- aftershave
- bath fizzers
- body butter
- body mist
- body spray
- body wash
- bubble bath
- candles
- cologne
- conditioner
- deodorant
- eau de cologne
- essential oils
- fragrance
- gel
- hand cream
- lip balm
- lotion
- lubes
- massage oil
- moisturizer
- mouthwash
- perfume
- shampoo
- shower gel
- soap
- sprays
- sun cream
- sunscreen
- toothpaste

Scents considered sensual or attractive:

(while some people may love a certain scent, others may loathe it. Go with your characters!)

- bergamot
- cinnamon
- citrus
- flowers
- fresh-cut grass
- ginger
- ginseng
- honeysuckle
- jasmine
- lavender
- lemon
- lilac
- lilies
- mint
- orange
- patchouli
- peaches
- pine
- pink grapefruit
- raspberries
- roses
- saffron
- sandalwood
- strawberry
- sweat
- vanilla
- ylang ylang

Places to have sexual encounters

Your imagination could take you anywhere, but here is a list of common, popular, exciting, and unusual places where encounters could take place.

- a balcony
- a bar
- a bath
- a bathroom (public/private/on an airplane/ on a train)
- a beach
- a bed (not necessarily your own)
- a car
- a caravan
- a cave
- a chair
- a club
- a concert
- a deserted building
- a desk
- a field
- a forest/ woodland
- a garden
- a gazebo
- a golf course
- a greenhouse
- a gym

The Ins and Outs of a Sex Scene

- a hallway
- a hammock
- a horse trailer
- a hot tub
- a hotel room
- a jacuzzi
- a kitchen
- a lift/ elevator
- a lighthouse
- a living room
- a locker room
- a lodge/ cabin/ boathouse
- a mattress
- a motel
- a movie theatre/ cinema
- a park bench
- a party
- a pier
- a pool table
- a pool/ poolside
- a rooftop
- a sauna
- a shed
- a shop
- a shower (indoor/ outdoor/ public/ private)

The Ins and Outs of a Sex Scene

- a sofa
- a stairwell
- a table
- a tennis court
- a tent
- a tractor
- a train
- a trampoline
- a waterbed/ airbed
- a waterfall
- a wet room
- an alleyway
- an ice-hotel
- an igloo
- at a famous landmark
- at a wedding
- backstage
- beside a river
- in a sleeping bag
- in front of a fireplace
- in the sea
- in the wilds
- on a car hood
- on a ship/ boat/ yacht
- on satin sheets
- on the grass

- on the set of a play/ movie
- on top of a mountain
- on top of a washing machine
- onstage
- the back of a limo
- the back of a taxi
- the floor
- the office
- up against a tree

Phrases to modify and enhance places:

(Mix and match with the above locations. E.g. in a hammock at midnight or on top of a mountain at sunrise)

- after dark
- after hours
- at midnight
- at night
- at sunrise
- at sunset
- during a break
- during a firework show
- during a heatwave
- during a storm (rain/ snow/ thunder)
- during the day
- during working hours
- early morning
- in a crowded area
- in a heavy fog/ mist
- on a business trip
- on a road trip
- on holiday
- under the stars
- while friends are there too
- with curtains open
- with the lights on
- with the windows open

Clothing & Toys

Clothing

(Some clothing is intrinsically sexy, other items may be removed seductively or enhance a person's attractiveness)

- ball gown
- bathing suit
- bikini
- blouse
- boob tube
- boots
- boxer shorts
- boxers
- bra
- brassiere
- briefs
- button-down shirt
- camisole
- chemise
- corset
- dinner jacket
- dress
- dress shirt
- earrings
- evening gown
- fur coat
- garters
- girdle
- glasses
- gown
- halter top
- high heels
- hosiery
- hot pants
- jeans
- jodhpurs
- kaftan
- kilt
- kimono
- knickers
- lab coat
- lapel
- leather jacket
- leotard
- lingerie
- miniskirt

- necklace
- nightgown
- nightshirt
- onesie
- panties
- pants
- pencil skirt
- petticoat
- polo shirt
- pajamas
- ring
- sandals
- sarong
- sheath dress
- shift
- shirt
- shorts
- slip
- stockings
- suit
- sundress
- sunglasses
- suspenders
- swimsuit
- teddy
- tie
- tights
- T-shirt
- tube top
- tux
- tuxedo
- underclothes
- underwear
- vest
- wedding gown
- wetsuit

Sex Toys

- anal beads
- butt plugs
- cock rings
- dildos
- kegel balls
- massagers
- penis sleeves
- pumps
- vibrators

The Ins and Outs of a Sex Scene

The Ins and Outs of a Sex Scene

Printed in Great Britain
by Amazon